The Only Email Marketing System That Grants You Power to Send <u>Unlimited</u> Offers to Your List!

Customers on Demand

How to Multiply Your Health Product Sales without Spending a Dime on Paid Traffic

By Levi Heiple

Customers on Demand

To Russell Brunson, who introduced me to the power of stories and helped a clueless college grad get started on a good career.

Preface (To Be Read)

Thank you for purchasing **Customers on Demand**. Welcome aboard!

Here's my big promise:

This book will teach you the only email marketing system that grants you power to send *unlimited* offers to your list.

You are likely already familiar with some email tactics and strategies. But this book will get to the *root* of what your email subscribers want and why they buy. It will show you how to write emails that both *entertain* and present compelling information about your product ("info-tainment").

I've written this book specifically for using email to sell health products such as supplements, health newsletters, or other similar offers. That said, the strategies I write about can be applied in *any* market and used on *any* medium. So don't limit yourself!

Most entrepreneurs take the hard path to making more sales. When they want more revenue they build a new funnel, do a new product launch, or some other kind of promotion. The problem with this strategy is

9 times out of 10, the new promotion will fail!

Even world-class copywriters fail more often than they succeed when creating new promotions. This isn't to say you shouldn't try to create that next million-dollar funnel, I'm only saying there is an *easier* and more *immediate* way to multiply your sales.

It's expensive to test new ideas. But, when done correctly, email allows you to send unlimited messages to your market with zero risk of losing money. That's the power of infotainment. Not only will your messages be fun to read, but you can multiply your sales without having to lose a dime on advertising!

Most people do email wrong. That's why they either fail to get results or they "churn and burn" through their list. But by time you finish this short book, you'll understand how to send emails *every day* in a way that makes both your readers and your bank account happy.

I've done my best to lay out all the basics you need so you can immediately apply this to your business. If you have any questions, or are interested in having this system implemented as a done-for-you service, don't hesitate to email me at Levi@LeviTheEmailGuy.com or leave a voicemail at 208-495-6119.

About the Author

Levi Heiple is an email copywriter who has written for Russell Brunson (ClickFunnels), Perry Marshall, and many others. He now specializes in writing daily "infotaining" emails for the health market.

Contents

1. The System (p. 6)

Part I: Understanding Your Perfect Audience
2. How to Ethically Steal Your Competitors' Money (p. 11)
3. Misery Loves Company (p. 17)

Part II: Crafting the Perfect Message
4. The 5 Message Strategies for Multiplying Email Sales (p. 25)
5. The Obvious Question (p. 30)
6. The Sob Story (p. 38)
7. The Horror Story (p. 45)
8. The Customer's Journey (p. 51)
9. The Dopamine Hit (p. 59)

Part III: Making the Perfect Pitch
10. The Daily "Mini-Sales Letter" (p. 65)
11. Sex Up the Offer (p. 71)
12. "Vision Drives Decision" (p. 76)
13. No B.S. (p. 79)
14. Don't Kill the Sale (p. 86)

Part IV: Resources
15. How to Get Started (p. 90)
16. Author Contact Information (p. 92)

~1~
The System

If you only read one chapter from this book, read this one!

I'm going to show you a system that will allow you to make sales *on demand* from your email list. The emails are very simple to write and fun to read. You don't have to worry about burning out your list.

And, perhaps best of all, what I'm going to show you is a helluva lot easier than product launches, or any other kind of promotion or sales funnel.

Why Most Companies Suck at Email

At its most basic level this book is about email marketing. Email marketing is about marketing to your email list (duh).

But really stop to think about that...

Most companies fail to get good results from their email marketing. And the reason is because...

> They aren't doing email *marke*ting!

Most companies try to *sell* to their email list, and that's why they burnout the list. Selling is when you talk about your product. People don't want to read about your product all the time; they want to read about their problems.

When you talk about your market's problems, that's when you're doing marketing. And people have an *unlimited appetite* for marketing when it's done right.

If you can write about your market's problems in a way that is fun to read, then you can briefly connect your products to the solution, and you will send a flood of pre-sold readers to your sales page every day.

This is not unlike the concept of talk radio, where the host is talking about what's going on in the world. They're talking about problems that their listeners are concerned about. And throughout the show they plug their products. It's a brief and casual mention. It's not hard selling; it's fluent, and non-evasive, but very effective.

The Only 3 Things That Matter

One of the most important marketing insights I ever learned was from "attraction marketing" specialist Tyson Zahner. In a nutshell, what he taught was there are only 3 core activities that move the needle when it comes to marketing & sales:

1. **Understanding your perfect audience**
2. **Crafting the right messages**
3. **Putting offers in front of them**

All other marketing activity is a waste if it doesn't serve at least one of those three goals.

The system I'm going to show you in this book perfectly serves the above three goals.

I'm going to show you how to **find insights about your perfect audience** that can be quickly spun into emails.

I'm going to show you how to **craft messages that guarantee you're never boring** to your (potential) customers.

Finally, I'm going to show you how to **put offers in front of your market every single day** so you can easily multiply your sales.

The remainder of the book will go into details and examples on how to do each step of this system. For now, just know that all you only need three things to execute this system:

1. An email list (either customers or newsletter subscribers)
2. A broadcasting system to send the emails (e.g. Drip, ConvertKit, Aweber, etc.)
3. A simple sales page (e.g. ClickFunnels, Gumroad, Amazon page, etc.)

That's it. This is the simplest way in the world to make sales.

Embrace Imperfection

The emails you send do not have to be perfect. In fact, imperfection feels more personal and is even more effective. Do NOT try to polish these messages. Don't try to sound professional. Keep them casual and personal. Write them as if you were writing to a friend.

And don't get hung up on the performance metrics of each email. A lot of people like to look at their open rates, or their click through rates, or even their individual sales from each email. This is a big mistake because

Your sales trends are the only metric that matters

It's impossible to look at one email and judge whether your messages are working. One email may have pre-sold them but they didn't take action that day. Maybe they wait until a deadline. Or they buy when you send the next email. Personally, there's been many times when I'll read one email and get excited about a product but I won't buy because I'm on my phone or busy working or whatever. When the next email shows up, I barely even read it. It just reminded me that I wanted to buy the product. So I just scroll down to the link and buy.

This is why you can't get hung up on the metrics for each individual email. It's the *cumulative* effect that you want to track. You don't want to miss the important trends like whether or not your sales are going up or down by trying to over-optimize the metrics from each individual email.

My Big Promise

If you follow this system I layout in this book you should be able to double your sales from your email list, for the simple reason that you'll be sending more offers that your list will actually read instead of ignore. The more people read your offers, the more people will go to your sales page and the more sales you'll make. It's as simple as that.

Let's dive in...

Part I:

Understanding Your Perfect Audience

~2~
How to Ethically Steal Your Competitors' Money

Did you know your competitors are sitting on a goldmine of insights and aren't even using it?

Wouldn't it be great if you could ethically "steal" that gold for your own business?

Well, you can if you know where to look and what to look for.

The "gold" I'm talking about is the market insights you can glean from your competitor's product pages.

Market research is the "unsexy" part of this business. Everyone wants to get to the "good stuff." Put up a sales page. Send some emails. Make some money.

But taking the time to understand your buyer is just as much a revenue generating activity as sending out offers. In fact, **if you don't understand the buyer's point of view, everything else is a waste.**

Thankfully, the internet makes it easy to understand your buyer's world. They post it publically for anyone to read. If only people knew what a goldmine this free information was!

Then again, it's probably good they don't know. Let's keep it a secret competitive advantage between you and me.

So let's talk about how to quickly get up to speed with your potential buyers. I'll show an example in the supplement space first. Then I'll show an example of how to do it if you're selling an information product (like a newsletter.)

How to Find Marketing Gold on Your Competitor's Amazon Page

Head over to Amazon and type in what you think your prospects would search for if they wanted to buy your product. (You can use Amazon's auto-suggest feature to find the most popular search terms.)

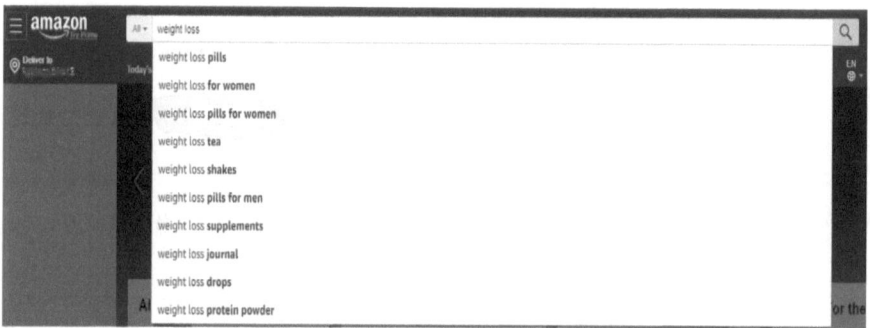

"Weight loss pills for women." That looks promising. Let's check it out…

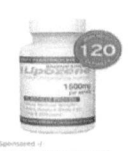     

Any one of these products can be a goldmine for buyer insights. For now, I'll pick the "Burn XT" supplement which is (at the time of this writing) "Amazon's Choice."

(NOTE: You do not have to use YOUR product listing to do this research. In fact, your competitor's product can be even more valuable. You'll see why in a second…)

I'm going to scroll down to the review section. I'm only going to look at the 5 and 1 star reviews. These are the *passionate* buyers. We don't care about people who tried and thought "Meh. It's okay. Probably won't order again."

We want to address the reasons why people either LOVE or HATE the product.

Let's start with the good stuff. What we're looking for is EMOTIONAL information:

☆☆☆☆☆ **Waited over a month and wow great overall product**
June 10, 2018
Verified Purchase

So to start this is my girlfriends account im a 25 year old male using the product. Body history i use to be 5 percent bodyfat on a strict keto diet at 5'9 215 pounds i was a avid body lifter since high school. About 5 years ago i was injured in a work accident that shattered my wrist in pieces and put me out for a year. Then only after a few months of being back to normal before i could even get my gym grind back on i was in a motorcycle accident that tore 3 of 4 ligaments in my right knee and reshattered my wrist in even more places. I became depressed fell off my diet! mcdonalds was my new and cheapest friend). I pretty much neglected my body since then became 230lbs at over 23% body fat. I live in florida and work outside detailing boats and this summer has started off brutal. My crew and i are always tired, hungry and mentally drained however none of us are truely in shape or have the energy at the end of the day to go to the gym. I decided I needed to get my body back and get my health up. I completely cut out fast food (i eat better not great most of my grocery shopping is done at walmart and i do still eat certain processed foods). Started fasting from 2 to 11 and going to the gym at a 3 days on 1 day off cycle with 10 min of warm up cardio at a 140 to 150bpm do my weights and finish with 5 min of cardio at a 170 to 180bpm. Right into my first week i was extremely tired slacking at work mentally not there and always always hungry to the point where it hurt and my guys would here my stomach growl. I had actually heard a radio advertisement for force factor xt but i always reseach my supplements and came across this a way healthier organic more reliable and better reviewed product plus free 1 day shipping and i needed it ASAP if i was gonna keep to my new lifestyle hahah. I have now been taking these 1 in the morning between 6 and 8 and 1 in the evening between 12 and 2 for over a month and a half.... Im absolutely mind blown how well they really work my appetite is suppressed not to bug me in the morning but not so much that i have trouble getting 3000 calories in during my fasting period. As for my mind these things are like limitless pills im very focused alert and awake im able to guide my crew and manage without missing a beat on top of the nice energy boost i feel in the gym. I can honestly say that im both giving work and gym 100 percent every day. As for the body i now weigh 208 but dont let that scare you as i said i was a body builder and im focused on muscle gains. My waist line has dropped over 9 inches and my definition and size is coming along great im right around 15 percent body fat. If your afraid of losing muscle i havent hit that problem yet its actually helped me gain with the improved energy and focus in the gym. Ive actually recommended it to my entire team. I feel great and im starting to look great. However my one and only concern is i have developed a slight dependency if i miss taking one i get a migraine and feel very sluggish and ran down. I believe this is just because i work 6 days week 8 to 10 hours a day in the blazing sun and am going to the gym pretty hard core most people start with just 3 days a week but none the less it is something to keep in mind. I would definitely and highly recommend giving this product a try its not a super pill i would still recommend a decent diet and exercise but it helps and boosts your efforts and rewards along the way and allows you to grind and push yourself beyond your normal limits which is essential in body development everyone hits platos its just figuring out how to overcome them 👍

Look at all that marketing gold!

"I was injured in a work accident that shattered my wrist and put me out for a year."

"Tired of slacking at work… mentally not there and always always hungry to the point where it hurt."

"Absolutely mind blown how well they really [well] my appetite is suppressed not to bug me in the morning."

"Only concern is I have developed a slight dependency."

Turning Customer Reviews into Product Hooks

Each of these little nuggets could be turned into a hook for your product:

"I know of this guy who was in a work accident that shattered his wrist for a year. He couldn't go to the gym for a whole year. Even the most self-disciplined among us can get off track when life happens. That's why an appetite suppressant can be a great way to get back on track."

"Hunger pangs can be a major distraction. It's hard to focus on your work. Your manager thinks you're slacking, when really you're just trying to avoid overeating!"

"Our supplement is specifically designed to suppress your appetite. That means when you wake up in the morning, you won't have that obnoxious angry stomach demanding you feed it!"

"Is our supplement dangerous to be addicted to? Many users find it works so well in suppressing their appetite, they worry if it's safe to be taking every day..."

All this stuff is WAY more interesting than simply talking about your product. It centers everything in their world. You're talking about THEIR problems so it's automatically interesting to them.

This is a very easy way to generate ideas for an infinite number of emails. Just find an emotional hot button, write about it, then plug your product.

Your prospects will love to read it because it's 95% about them. You only talk about yourself at the end, as the obvious solution to their problem.

This is one of the reasons you can get away with sending them a "mini-sales letter" every day. I'll get into this more later, but for now I'll just leave you with this quote from the "World's Most Feared Negotiator", Jim Camp:

"You're always safe when you're in their world."

Some marketers worry about whether they're sending too many promotions. Others don't care and just pitch all the time.

But the secret is to keep everything rooted in their world. Don't talk about your product, talk about their problems. That's how you "get away" with selling every day.

~3~
Misery Loves Company

The internet is a marketer's dream come true.

Where else but online do millions of people publicly post their random frustrations and problems for the world to read?

If you're a savvy marketer, you should recognize what a goldmine this is.

Marketing is connecting problems to a solution. And if people are openly posting their problems for everyone (including you) to read, that makes your job as a marketer a helluva lot easier.

There is one site in particular that people congregate to discuss their frustrations for almost every problem imaginable.

I'm talking about **Reddit.com**.

The site is organized into "subreddits" that revolve around particular topics. Honestly, people mostly just go there to complain and vent and gossip about the latest news. So if you want to maintain a positive mindset, I don't recommend looking for solutions there.

But as someone with a product (solution) to offer, it's a goldmine of insights you can use to sell your product.

Spinning Misery Into Profits

Here's an example how to take the frustrations people are venting on Reddit and channel it into selling more of your product. As you'll see, we're going to do this in an empathetic way. It's not about *making* people miserable so we can sell them more drugs (there's another industry you can get into if you want to do that.)

First, you want to think of a health problem someone might have that your product could solve.

Here's a subreddit called "loseit" (as in "Lose the Fat.")

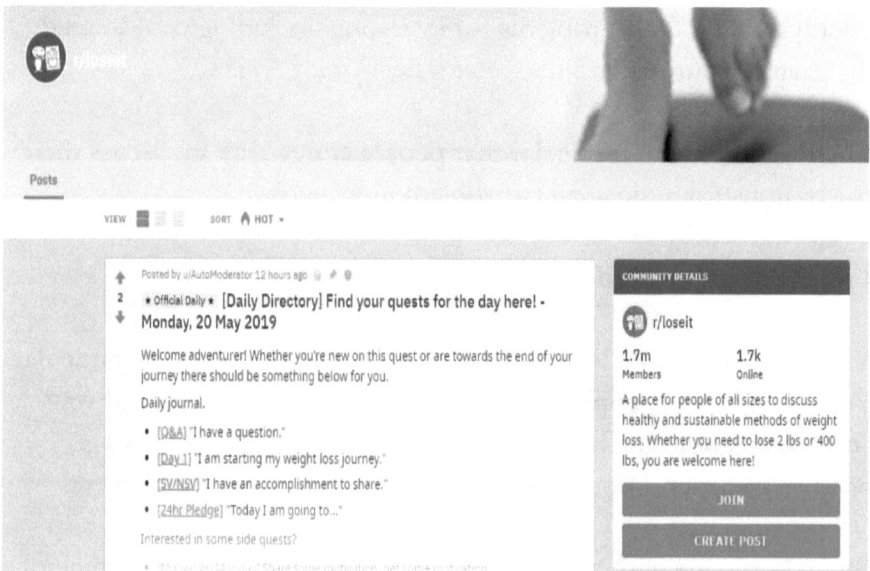

Weight loss is something almost *any* health product could help solve.

When I'm first visiting one of these forums, I'll sort the posts by "Top." This will show the most upvoted posts. Reddit is cool because, not only do you get to read the post and comments, you can also get a feel for how well it resonated with the audience based on the number of upvotes.

Upvoting is a private way for people to say *"Yes! This is so true! People need to read this!"*

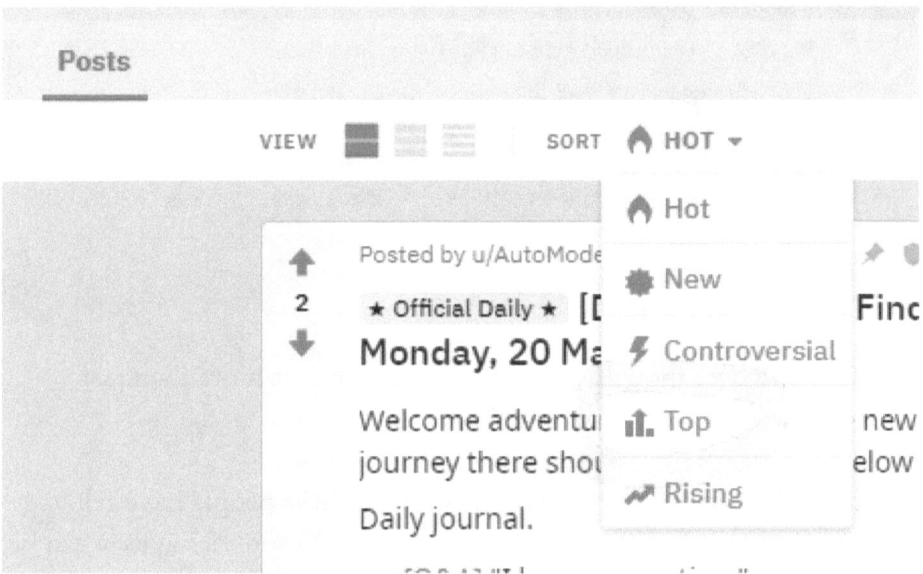

I usually filter the posts by "Past Year." This gives me a wide enough period to find the big hot-button issues, but still be current with where the conversations at. Markets evolve over time in what they know and believe, so if you're addressing "old news" you'll appear out of touch and untrustworthy.

Right away, I see a great theme for a marketing message:

> ↑ Posted by u/-life_starts_now- 235lbs lost - 29M - SW:605 CW:376 GW:205 9 months ago 4 ⓢ
> 20.9k
> ↓   · NSV: Today my doctor told me that he was proud of me. It's the first time I can remember anyone ever saying that to me.
>
> Hello everyone. This is my first post here. I've been commenting a little but never posted before.
>
> I started seeing my doctor in February when I was 530 pounds I had already lost 75 pounds at this point but I'm not sure if he really believed me when I told him. He asked me what my health goals were and I told him "I want to lose 100 pounds before I turn 29 in October. He told me "well, that's a lot of weight" and never said much else about it.
>
> Today I went in and got weighed at 398 pounds. I beat my goal by 32 pounds and 2 months. When he looked at my chart he said "wow, you did it! I'm really proud of you, keep it up!"
>
> I honestly teared up as soon as he walked out of the room, because this was the first time

Have you ever thought about how weight loss is more than just losing weight?

It's about personal achievement. Many of these people have felt like failures their whole lives. They just want to do something they can be proud of.

It's never about your product for them. It's about transforming their lives. You've got to meet them where they're at in their personal journey.

The Easiest Way in the World to Promote Your Product

Here's an example how you could turn a story like the one above into a (non-sleazy) promotion for your product.

Today, I read a story that truly moved me.

A woman started seeing her doctor. She weighed 530 pounds.

She told her doctor, "I want to lose 100 pounds before I turn 29 in October (it was February at the time.)

The doctor didn't seem to believe her. He simply said, "well, that's a lot of weight."

But when she weighed herself in August she was down to 392 pounds. She beat her goal by 32 pounds and 2 months!

When the doctor looked at her chart, he said, "Wow! You really did it. I'm really proud of you, keep it up!"

The doctor probably had no idea how much that compliment meant to her.

It was the first time in her life anyone told her they were proud of her.

That's the thing about losing weight…

It's not just about "getting healthy." It's about proving to yourself that you can do something. Giving a silent "FU" to all your doubters.

And then accepting the (well-earned) praise when you finally achieve your goal.

You're probably curious how this woman lost so much weight.

She started out by counting calories. First she limited herself to under 3800 calories… then under 3000 calories per day and so on until she got down to around 1800 calories a day.

She used intermittent fasting to make the calorie reduction easier.

So the plan is simple in theory.

The tough part, is you've got to have the self-discipline to avoid eating when you've got a "rumbling in your tumbling."

That's why, for many people, an appetite suppressor can be a useful aid in reaching your weight loss goals.

Our [PRODUCT NAME] is specially formulated to…. [BRIEFLY PLUG YOUR PRODUCT]

You can get a free sample bottle here (just cover the shipping):

[LINK TO SALES PAGE]

I whipped up that email just by reading a single Reddit post. That's how simple it is to find new content ideas.

How to Get Unlimited Ideas from Reddit

You can do this all day long with Reddit. Find a post. Paraphrase the story/problem. Plug your product.

Honestly, you could do this *every day* and most of your audience would never tire of reading your "mini-sales letters." You're writing about *their* world and their world is never boring to them.

Later, I'm going to cover ways you use more variety in your emails. You don't necessarily want to just do the same thing every time. But even if all you did was execute this simple Reddit hack, you'd be light years ahead of most of your competition.

And you don't have to limit yourself to weight loss. If there's a health problem, there's a subreddit about it. You have an endless supply of ideas at your fingertips.

At the least, you should be checking in once in a while with the top posts on the forums relevant to your market. You want to get a feel for the problems they're having, the language they're using, what kind of stories are inspiring them, etc.

This might feel like wasting time. We're conditioned to think of reading social media as a low value activity. But when you're eavesdropping in on conversations your *market* is having, it's probably the most profitable activity you can do… provided you have a system in place to turn those insights into gold. That's what I'm going to cover next.

Part II:

Crafting the Perfect Message

~4~
The 5 Message Strategies for Multiplying Email Sales

The 5 message strategies I'm going to introduce you to are designed so that you can send as many offers as you want to your list without burning them out.

The reason these strategies work is because you are *empathizing* with your customers and *inspiring* them to make changes in their life instead of just talking about your product. You can do this in a way that comes across as very conversational and natural... like a knowledgeable friend. It's not sleazy in any way, so your readers are going to enjoy reading it. But you still get to plug your product at the end.

Another advantage of these strategies is it's going to help you avoid being dependent on a single source of traffic or sales.

Platforms like Google, Facebook or Amazon might decide at any time they don't like your product for whatever reason and boot you off their platform. But the message strategies I'm going to teach you can work on any platform, so you don't have to be reliant on any single platform to send you your traffic.

I'm going to be talking about email, obviously, but keep in mind that you can use this on any platform: Google ads, Facebook, blog posts, even direct mail. The fundamentals are all the same.

The advantage of email, of course, is that if you are using paid traffic, you're going to get better results from that traffic if you have an effective email system. You can sell a lot more of your product on the backend and get a better ROI on your traffic.

Most "Marketers" Don't Have Anything to Say

What is a message?

It's a simple, but profoundly important question.

Here's how most companies do "marketing":

They think, *"Hey, let's sell something!"* So they put out an ad or send out an email. And *all they do is talk about the offer.* There's no compelling reason to read it unless they already wanted to buy the product.

That's not marketing. (Well, technically it is, but it's about as low-level as it gets. You're basically just sending a few people a reminder that they wanted to buy your product while simultaneously annoying everyone else.) This strategy might work fine for restaurants and local stores. But if you expect to sell supplements, newsletters, or any other health-related product, you're going to need a more sophisticated strategy. Just sending out a discount code with a deadline ain't gonna cut it.

When I talk about a **message**, I mean something that's worth reading in and of itself. As the "Greatest Living Copywriter", Gary Bencivenga put it, *"Your advertising should be valuable in and of itself."*

That's the difference between **marketing vs. selling**.

**Selling is when you are talking
about *your* product.**

**Marketing is when you're talking
about *their* problems.**

People don't like to read sales material unless they are ready to buy the product. That's when it's appropriate to talk about your products. When they're ready to buy, tell them about all the wonderful features and benefits your product offers. That's why we send people to a *sales* page. If you're selling a health supplement, can talk about the ingredients and how it's clinically proven to be effective and all that good stuff. Or if you're selling a newsletter, you might tease some of the content that they'll find in there so they want to try it out.

Selling is a necessary part of the equation. People need to learn about your product before they buy.

But before anyone's ready to buy, you need to *market* to them. People don't read sales material for fun, but they'll read *marketing* content all day long if it's done right.

The reason they love to read marketing is because the content is all about and their problems. It's talking about their world, their frustrations, their struggles, so it's always going to be interesting to them.

Five Ways to Never Be Boring Again!

There are five basic messaging strategies you can use. If you frame your marketing messages in one of these themes, it's almost guaranteed to be interesting to your reader. The five themes are:

1. The Obvious Question
2. The Sob Story
3. The Horror Story
4. The Customer's Journey
5. The Dopamine Hit

I'm going to get into detail on each of these strategies later. But for now, I just wanted to give you a quick tease :-)

The reason these themes work is because they leverage a communication style called "infotainment." This is a term I learned from the great email copywriter, Ben Settle (and I believe he learned it from Matt Fury.)

The basic idea behind infotainment is this:

People can tolerate unlimited amounts of marketing if it's entertaining to read.

If the writing style is conversational or even funny (or at least fun to read), people aren't going to mind that you're marketing to them. People will spend hours watching Netflix or scrolling through their Facebook timeline, and they never get tired of it because it's not taxing on their brains. And those mediums are full of marketing and propaganda messages. But it's fun to consume. People do it just do it to chill out.

The human mind has an unlimited capacity for consuming entertainment.

If you blend entertainment with your marketing, your promotions become fun to read. Many won't even realize it's a promotion per se.

And if people like to read your stuff, it means you can send out more offers.

If your list is large enough, you don't even have to write the emails yourself. You can hire one guy to build your list and another guy to send the emails while you sit back and watch your bank account grow.

Regardless whether you do it yourself or outsource the work, if you follow the strategy that I lay out, it is highly probable that you will **double or triple your sales**.

The reason I can say that is not because of some kind of "secret sauce" or mystical mind-programming like NLP or anything like that.

It's just common sense.

The more fun your content is to read, the more often people will open your emails and read your message. And the more they read it, the more often they'll see your offers in a positive way.

Your sales increase simply because more people read your offer.

Sound good? Alright, let's dive in...

~5~
The Obvious Question

Wouldn't it be great if you could eliminate the competition in your customer's mind and position your product as the *only* viable solution?

That's exactly what you can do when you use what I call the "Obvious Question" strategy.

What you're going to do is position yourself as a trusted advisor instead of someone just pitching their wares saying, *"Buy my stuff! Look how great our product is!"* You're going to help your prospects become an *informed consumer*, even if they don't buy your product or decide not to buy that day.

Another benefit of this strategy is you'll reduce your refund rates. Oftentimes, especially in our consumerist American culture, we'll buy things simply because it's on sale or because we had a fear of missing out. Many times we buy things without fully understanding what we're getting. Or maybe we had false expectations of what the product did and didn't do our due diligence because we were acting on impulse. That's why people end up refunding good products (at least the honest people... there is a class of people known as "serial refunders", but that's an entirely different topic.)

This will also help you reduce a lot of your back end customer service. A lot of times people buy a product, without fully understand what it does because they weren't educated up front on what they're buying. So you have the added expense of customer service reps having to explain basic things about the product to new customers.

And consider this:

For every question someone asks *after* the purchase, how many people decided NOT to buy because they had that same question *before* they purchased?

A little bit of preemptive customer service can actually help you make more sales.

And if you're the only company that directly addressed their question, then you're the only company they feel safe buying from.

You're Just One Question Away...

When I say the "Obvious Question", I'm talking about that one lingering concern or question people have before they become ready to buy your product (or even your *type* of product.)

Often times, these little "hang ups" might seem obvious to you as the seller, but they're important concerns for the interested buyer. Leave them unaddressed, and the sale is killed.

For example, let's say you're selling a liver cleanse supplement. Here are some questions people might have before they're ready to make the purchase:

- *"How long does it take to work?"*
- *"How can you tell if it's working?"*
- *"What do the capsules taste like?"*
- *"What are the ingredients? Are they vegetarian?"*

These are simple questions that are easy to answer. But few companies think to address them, let alone use them as a lead for a marketing message.

How to Read Your Prospects' Minds

One difficulty you'll run into when trying to implement this strategy is that customers typically won't reach out to you and ask the question on their mind. A few of them do, and that's helpful. But most people ponder in silence and never ask. Maybe they're afraid of sales pressure or maybe they're just too lazy to ask. It could be a variety of reasons. But very rarely will people reach out and tell you what their real concerns are about purchasing your product.

There's few things more frustrating as a marketer than knowing you have a great product, but not knowing why people aren't buying it.

Thankfully, there are some simple ways that you can shed some light on this mysterious black box.

One simple thing you can do is you could head over to Amazon.com and look at product pages that are similar to yours. There's a section on each product page called customer Q&A. This is where people will anonymously post questions that they had about the product before they click the add to cart button.

Customers on Demand

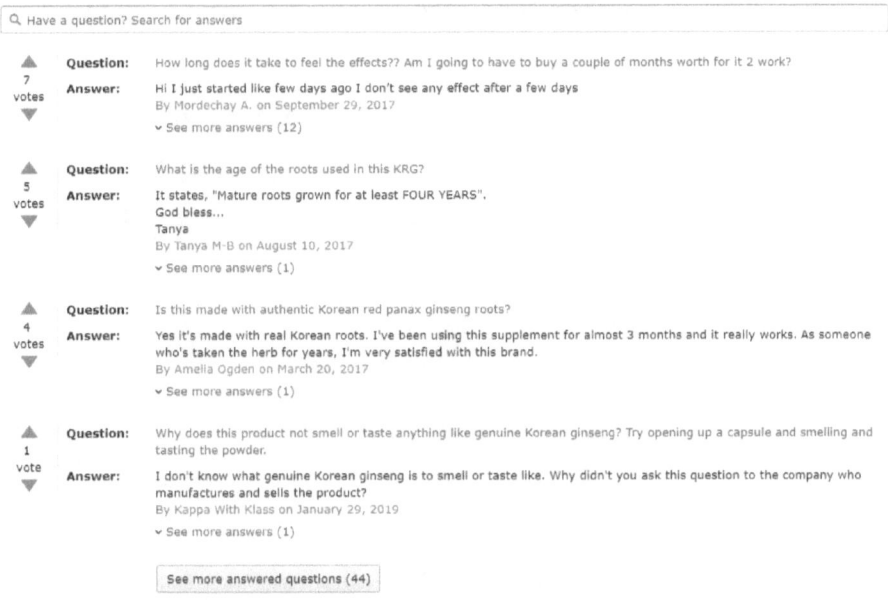

This is really valuable information because you're literally getting to read the customer's mind *right before they make a buying decision*. So you can find out exactly what is on their mind. What's that last little hang up that's preventing them from clicking the "Add to Cart" button?

Each of these questions can be turned into a compelling email.

> **Subj: How long does Ginseng take to work?**
>
> I recently read some customer reviews on Amazon for a popular Ginseng supplement.
>
> People were asking, "How long does this take to work? I've been taking these supplements for 3 weeks and haven't felt a thing!"

33

Customers on Demand

This was surprising because the product had thousands of positive reviews. (Whether they were paid reviews or not, I don't know.)

I can't speak one way or another for the validity of the product, but what I can tell you is this:

Many Ginseng supplements contain hardly any real Ginseng!

It won't take you 3 weeks to tell whether the supplement is working. Ginseng starts working as soon as it hits the bloodstream (typically within 15-30 minutes.)

Most who take Ginseng feel an increase in mental alertness and concentration as soon as it hits their bloodstream.

In addition to the time, you can tell if a supplement contains real Ginseng by the taste. Ginseng roots have a bitter spicy taste with earthy undertones. It's not a strong taste, but if you break open one of the capsules and put it on your tongue, you should be able to taste the Ginseng.

If all your tasting is salt and rice powder?

Well, then that's probably all it is.

Don't be deceived. Trust your senses.

I can tell you all this in full confidence because our [PRODUCT] is the real deal.

Break open a capsule and you can TASTE the earthy undertones of the authentic Korean red panax Ginseng roots we put in each capsule.

Grab a trial bottle here and taste the difference for yourself:

LINK

Another thing you could look at is negative reviews on Amazon. Look at the people that bought products similar to yours. You can look at health supplements or if you're selling a newsletter, you can look at books that address similar themes. But look at the negative reviews (e.g. one and two star reviews).

Find out why they did not like the product. It will usually be because they had a false expectation about how the product would perform. In many cases, it's not even that the product was bad, it's just that the customer had false expectations.

You can make a list of these false expectations and address it in an email that spins the false expectation into an opportunity for your readers to make an informed purchase.

> **Subj: Can turmeric give you the runs?**
>
> I recently read about a poor guy who complained about having nausea and horrible diarrhea after taking a turmeric supplement.
>
> This is unfortunate, but it's not necessarily a problem with the turmeric. The majority of people can take turmeric without any significant side effects. But some people do report upset stomach, nausea, dizziness, or diarrhea.
>
> It's no different with trying any new supplement or diet. Your body might need an adjustment period.
>
> If you're concerned about it, talk to your doctor. In many cases, you'll probably be told to wait it out and let your body adjust.
>
> Also, it should go without saying, but make sure you get a turmeric supplement that is pure turmeric. One clever trick some

supplement companies pull is they advertise how the supplement contains all these other vitamins and minerals....

But what they're really saying is *"We added a bunch of useless cheap filler in order to maximize our profits. You're hardly getting any turmeric at all, but if you don't read the label, you won't know the difference! Ha ha ha..."*

Honestly, some of these companies make me sick how they dupe consumers.

With our [COMPANY] supplements, we take every measure to ensure we are transparent with our consumers.

Check the label for yourself:

[LINK TO PRODUCT PAGE]

The above email uses an old copywriting strategy called "making the skeleton dance." Take a negative about your product (potential side effects) and spin it into a positive (side effects means it's real; your body is adjusting.)

A final tactic you can use to get ideas is to simply send out an email to your list and just ask them *"what is your number one question about _____?"* (e.g. *"What is your number one question about weight loss?" "What is your number one question about appetite suppressants?"* Whatever type of product you're selling.)

The 50% Rule

There's a great rule of thumb I learned from Ken McCarthy, the "founding father" of Internet marketing. He said that if you have a list (email or direct mail), expect that **50% of that list will never buy no matter what you do.** These people signed up just because they wanted the freebie and they're too lazy to unsubscribe or they just like the free tips or whatever.

Then about **1-2% of your list will be your hyper-responsive buyers**. These are the ones that they'll just buy it simply because it's a good offer. They don't really need much persuasion. Give them an offer and they're in. These people are also on a lot of other lists and buying a lot of other products in your industry as well.

So that means

48% to 49% of your list are skeptics.

These people are not ready to buy because they have certain objections in their mind. They're more cautious than your hyper responsive buyers and need more time to make a decision.

The skeptical buyer is a huge untapped opportunity that I guarantee you most of your competitors are ignoring. You can address these skeptics simply by finding out what unanswered questions they have before they buy.

If you address these questions directly in your email marketing, you're going to convert many of these skeptics. But if you leave them unaddressed, there's a lot of sales you're leaving on the table.

Something to think about the next time you look over your sales stats. How many people were close to buying, but didn't because of one simple unaddressed question?

~6~
The Sob Story

In this chapter, I'm going to talk about turning other people's misery into your profit.

Of course, I don't mean doing this in an evil or manipulative way. You're going to do it in a way that helps better their life and alleviate their pain. But the reality is, especially in the health market, there wouldn't *be* a market if there wasn't pain and misery people were looking to escape from.

So that's one thing we have to accept: we are in the business of pain. Our market exists because of pain. People read our content and buy our products because of pain. And (most importantly) they want to know how to alleviate their pain.

You may have heard terms like "empathy-based marketing" and "leading with empathy."

> **Empathizing with someone means echoing back their pain and frustrations.**

When you empathize with someone, it creates an instant bond with them. People want to be heard, understood, and validated. Often times people have no one in their personal life who truly understands them or what they're going through. They feel very isolated. And marketers are often the only ones who take the time to understand what they're really going through.

Sad, but true.

So don't think of yourself as someone just trying to sell a product. **Think of yourself as a long-distance or virtual friend to these people who are suffering and looking for understanding and validation.**

And speaking from the business angle, leading with empathy allows you to control the narrative. You want them to be focusing on *their* problem so they can see your product as the obvious solution. You don't want them raising objections to claims you make about your product. To quite the great negotiator Jim Camp once more:

> "Vision drives decision."
> "Claims create objections."

You want to give them a *vision* of the problem they're experiencing. You want to talk about their problem even more articulately than they could express it themselves.

When you do this, you won't ever have to deal with writer's block or any shortage of ideas. There's only so much you can say about your product, but there's an *unlimited* number of problems you can talk about. People vent their problems online all the time; you'll never be short on ideas if you keep your eyes open.

Drama Sells

When I say a "Sob Story", I'm talking about finding a pain point or frustration that your market experiences and talking about that pain in a story format.

The truth is, **people don't buy products, they buy solutions to their problems.** As the old saying goes, *"don't tell me about your drill, tell me about the hole I want in my wall."*

Here's an example:

> **Subj: Too heavy to be on top**
>
> This is the "side effect" of weight gain that no one talks about...
>
> You're in bed with your wife and you're about to "get down to business."
>
> You position yourself on top but your wife tries to move you into another position. You ask her what's wrong.
>
> She hems and haws a bit... but you immediately know what the problem is:
>
> You're too heavy.
>
> She tries to apologize, but you tell her there's no need. You knew you were heavier than you'd ever been.
>
> You turn on the lamp and have a long chat. Then you put your PJs back on and go to sleep.
>
> Talk about a disappointing night!
>
> People who have never been overweight don't understand the struggle.
>
> It's not just about your health, it affects every area of your life. It's hard to "get it on" in the bedroom. You don't have the energy to play with your kids. You feel sluggish at work.
>
> It's the curse that keeps on taking.

And to make matters worse, greedy companies make sure your environment is set up with maximum temptations:

Chocolate bars, treats, and other junk food in front of your face every day at work.

Enticing food ads every time you sit down to chill with some TV or online videos.

Cultural traditions of eating fattening foods on almost every occasion.

The truth is, it takes a great act of willpower to say "NO!"

And you'll be hard pressed to find friends or family who will genuinely support your efforts. They may applaud your intentions, but when you start to make REAL progress? You might be surprised how quickly their support vanishes.

The good news is there are people out there like you who are committed to both shedding the weight and supporting others who are doing the same. We already have 257 members in our [GROUP NAME] who are taking back their life one pound at a time.

Members who join this week get our [BONUS GUIDE] for free. This guide includes a compilation of tasty and easy to make meals that our members have used to stay on track with their diets without having to eat bland "health" foods.

So if you've been on the fence about this, there's never been a better time to start! Join in time here:

LINK

Keep It Smooth

One of the difficulties you might run into when doing this is figuring out how to transition from the story into plugging your product. You don't want to come across like you're forcing it. That could kill your credibility.

You can see an example of how to do this in the email above. Here are some other ways I could have made the transition:

> *This is one of the reasons I created [GROUP NAME]. It's a community of like-minded people striving towards the same goal. This is NOT an impossible task. People are achieving it every day. And they're here to help you. Experience it for yourself here: LINK*
>
> *We talk about overcoming these obstacles every day inside [GROUP NAME]. You'd be surprised how many ways there are to do this. Get inside today: LINK*
>
> *Here's the deal: I don't have all the answers on how to deal with this. But others do. And there inside [GROUP NAME] sharing their hard-earned wisdom every day. If you're trying to do this alone, you're setting up your journey to be as difficult as possible. Join us for 1 month and see if it makes a difference: LINK*

Another difficulty people run into is not knowing how to tell a story. Maybe you know that your market experiences a certain frustration, but you don't know how to put it into a story.

Here's a very simple formula you can use for telling stories:

THE HERO'S 2 JOURNEYS

① Character
② Desire
③ Conflict

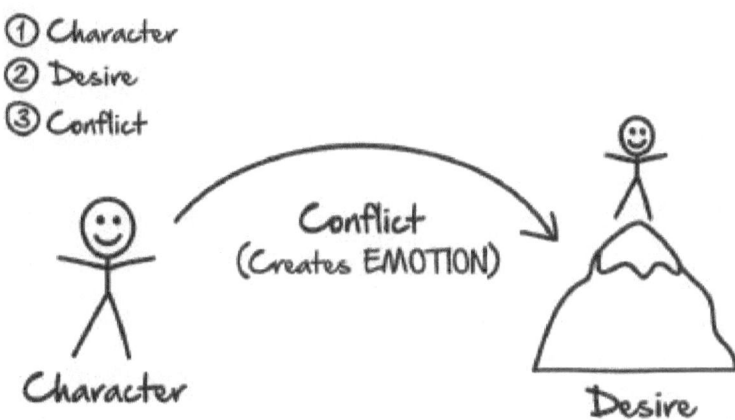

"The Hero's 2 Journeys" from Russell Brunson's *Expert Secrets*

I first learned this simple storytelling formula from Russell Brunson. I never realized how simple stories were until he broke it down like this.

Every story has three basic elements:

1. Character
2. Desire
3. Conflict

It's as simple as that.

A grandfather wants to play with his kids more but suffers from chronic fatigue.

A woman wants to spend more time at the beach but feels ashamed of her belly in a swimsuit.

A man wants to retire but he's worried about losing the insurance to cover medications for his diabetes.

These are all stories. They each have a character, a desire, and a conflict that is preventing them from achieving what they desire.

If you need to find some of your market's pain points to spin into stories, you can find an endless supply of this stuff on Reddit.com or other online forums related to problems your product can solve.

You've also got Amazon reviews. And don't underestimate good old-fashioned real-life conversations with your customers. Many people are happy to tell you about their problems.

I guarantee you that you will uncover dozens of pain points that your market is going through if you do some digging.

The reality today is that people are in a lot of pain due to bad health advice from conventional health authorities. This is especially true of the boomer generation. And while this pain isn't good, it is also a source of unlimited profit for you if you can ethically translate their painful experiences into bringing attention to the solution that you offer.

And when you do this, it's a win-win situation. You're helping people eliminate their pain and get their life back while making a "healthy" profit for yourself. (Sorry, had to throw at least one pun in there ;-)

~7~
The Horror Story

In this chapter, I'm going to show you how to "scare" your readers into buying your product without having to rely on deadlines, limited time offers, "limited supply", or anything like that. That stuff has its place. But if you do what I'm going to show you, you don't need to be hitting your list over the head with that stuff. People get sick of all those "Final Warning" emails and eventually tune you out if you overuse it.

The type of urgency I'm talking about is more subtle than blatant urgency or scarcity, but far more effective in the long-run.

You're going to give your readers a warning to **avoid a real danger in their life that can come from continuing down the path that they're on.** The most valuable advice you can give someone is what NOT to do. Positive advice can be ambiguous. You can't guarantee the outcome and people are (rightfully) skeptical.

But give advice to someone on what to *avoid* and it's easier to envision. You're giving them a definite painful scenario that they're going to avoid by following your advice. This allows you to bring immediate attention to the value of your product without having to "hard sell" it.

Like we talked about earlier, effective marketing is all about staying in their world. Talk about their problems. Then simply plug your product at the end.

And if you're selling a newsletter or other information product, this is a great way to overcome the common problem of *"how do I compete against free content online?"*

In theory, people could go to Google and find out whatever information is in your product. But, the real danger of doing that is following bad advice. People have no way of telling if the advice is good or if was written by a college graduate writing articles for $12/hour on topics he knows nothing about. (No joke. My first job out of college was doing that for an SEO company.)

A high-quality information product filters out the bad advice people might get from following misleading "free" advice on the internet. Create a vision of what's going to happen if they follow this bad advice. That's a great way to position your solution as the only way for them.

Scare Them to Save Them

A horror story is like the sob story we talked about previously. But the focus of the Horror Story is on the **damage done by a bad "solution."**

You're giving them a vivid picture of what happens when they follow uninformed advice.

Your market has to see your solution as the **only viable solution** for them before they're ready to buy. Your market is very aware of their health problem. Their experiencing the pain every day. They're researching solutions. They're fully aware that there are options out there that claim to be able to help them. But, they often suffer from analysis paralysis.

With so many options and so much jargon, your prospects will often avoid making a decision. The lack of clarity leads to indecision so they just drift along, suffering with their familiar pain as they go about their lives.

What you're doing with these "horror stories" is simplifying their decision for them. You're giving them clarity about which options are NOT good for them. Eventually, by **process of elimination, they see your product as the ONLY good choice.**

Here's an example how you can do this:

> **Subj: Mocked at the gym**
>
> Stuff like this infuriates me…
>
> One of my clients, Heather [not her real name], confessed to me that she was unmotivated to go to the gym because she was mocked the last time she went.
>
> She was a 5 foot woman. 130 pounds. Trying to get down to 100 pounds.
>
> She had been eating well and working out consistently. She decided she would up her game by going to the gym to do some strength training.
>
> She went over to the squat rack and pumped out 8 reps of 60 pounds. She was feeling proud of herself. It was a good start.
>
> While she was doing that, a super fit girl came over to the rack next to her and started pumping out 135+ pound squats. Her and her boyfriend kept staring and giggling every time Heather attempted her sets.

> She did her best to ignore them, but she obviously felt self-conscious.
>
> After a few minutes the boyfriend asked Heather to leave the rack for him to move "actual weight" instead of "baby weight."
>
> Heather felt incredibly embarrassed and teared up in front of everyone. She had always been self-conscious of working out as a short fat girl.
>
> Heather was so embarrassed by the experience that she hasn't been back to a gym in over 6 months even though she desperately wants to get fit and lose weight.
>
> I hate it when stuff like this happens. Truthfully, most people at the gym are friendly and encouraging.
>
> But it only takes one or two bad apples to spoil the whole barrel.
>
> Many of my clients have a fear of being mocked at the gym, especially when they're starting out and might be embarrassed by their weight or their lack of strength. This is understandable. Getting a little bit of "starting strength" can give you the confidence you need to hit the gym without feeling self-conscious.
>
> That's why I created [PRODUCT]. It's a strength training program for beginners that can be done at home with less than $100 worth of equipment...

In the example above, I took a common fear the market has (being mocked at the gym) and dramatized it with a story. If any reader was on the fence about whether to do a home workout program or go to a gym, a story like this would make the choice clear.

A Couple Warnings on Giving Warnings

There's a couple caveats you want to be aware of when using this strategy…

You want to **avoid using any of your competitors' names directly**. That could get you into legal trouble and could even bring some negative press on you that you don't want. Plus, it's risky to throw out claims about the quality of your competitor's products. You'd have to do a lot of research and fact-checking. Frankly, that energy is better spent understanding your market instead of trying to bring down a competitor.

The best way to tell these stories is to share stories about when things go wrong. Then explain *why* it went wrong. If it's necessary to mention a particular product, just say a "popular brand name supplement" or something like that. That will protect you from legal trouble. Plus, it's more persuasive anyways. Your reader will fill in the blank with whatever they think it is; by not calling out the brand directly, you could "take down" all your competitors by leveraging your reader's imagination!

I call it a "horror story" so it's memorable, but it doesn't always have to be graphic or dramatic. Sometimes it can be as simple as just taking a popular supplement and then getting a bad headache or stomach cramps or something like that. It doesn't always need to be anything particularly graphic or "scary.". (Although if it is, feel free to use it.)

The Horror Story is a simple way you can create some ethical urgency when you're sending out your offers. It'll help those who need your solution but are indecisive due to analysis paralysis.

~8~
The Customer's Journey

In this chapter, I'm going to show you how to turn a single testimonial into dozens, if not hundreds of sales.

Not only are you going to sell more product, but you will also be inspiring your readers to better their lives. There's no contradiction between contributing to a better world and selling your product if you do it like the way I'm going to show you.

I'm not talking about those lame one or two line testimonials you get from customers when you solicit feedback. Unfortunately, customers will rarely leave a great testimonial when asked. (People get writer's block and freeze up when they try to deliberately write something.) It's far better to

**Capture unsolicited praise and
spin it into stories that sell your product.**

This strategy will also allow you to circumvent the problem of competitors attacking your product by posting negative reviews on Amazon, or "reporting" you to one of those scam alert sites that shows up at the top of Google. People want social proof before they buy a product. And if they feel like the proof is lacking in your marketing message, they'll go to Google or Amazon to check you out. If they happen to see negative reviews on the top (fake or not), they're probably not going to buy.

But the way I'm going to show you allows you to circumvent all of that nonsense. In most cases, they won't even feel the need to look those things up because the social proof you give them is so powerful.

All this is the power of "The Customer's Journey."

Make Your Customer the Hero

The "Hero's Journey" is simply a success story where your customer is the hero.

This is different than the Sob Story where you are simply talking about a struggle that your market has. This story is more specific. It's about someone who was trying to achieve something then used your product to help get the results they desired.

> **People don't want a good product.
> They want a good life**.

If your product was one of the tools that helped them get that good life, then others will read that story. They'll be inspired and they'll immediately want the same product the hero used to get results.

Your customer doesn't care about you. They don't care about your product. They care about themselves and bettering their life.

Here's an example how to do this:

> Subj: Chronic fatigue… GONE!
>
> Terry writes in with another song of victory…
>
> *"I have been taking the Liver and Spleen supplements now for over 6 weeks and I just don't have enough words to describe*

how amazing I feel. I've been dealing with chronic fatigue, due to Hashimoto's hypothyroidism which is an autoimmune disease, for the past 5 years.

I am a busy, homeschooling, stay at home mom of 7 active children and have a husband who travels for work. Ain't nobody got time for chronic fatigue and neither do I!

My journey has been long In trying every natural option out there as well as working with my D.O. and my homeopathic doctor to put me on the road to a "normal" life. The benefits from these supplements have changed my life! I no longer dread getting out of bed in the morning nor do I look forward to the moment I can fall into bed at night and only hope to finally go to sleep.

I have more energy than I have had in years. My eyes feel bright and my mind is clear. My motivation to take on the day has returned and I couldn't be more grateful!

My children no longer ask me, " how do you feel today?" Because they can tell that I feel ALIVE again! Praising the Lord for bringing me to this site to find these AMAZING supplements!"
--

I can continue banging my drum every day about how we're all deficient in Vitamin A… how fruits & veggies alone don't cut it… or how our ancestors relied on organ meats for healthy skin, hair, gums, ligaments, tendons…

But at the end of the day, it's the stories of victory from real everyday people that show you the power of what I've been preaching.

Join Terry and thousands of others who are experiencing amazing health simply from adding this supplement to their daily morning ritual:

LINK

As you can see, Customer Hero stories are some of the easiest emails to do. Simply pull out a positive customer review or email, maybe break up the text a bit for easier reading, throw in a few comments at the end and *voila!*... a compelling email that will drive more sales!

Calling All Heroes...

The hardest part about pulling off the Hero's Journey strategy is finding enough good stories. The truth is that, even if you're product is good, most people won't get results. The statistic I here thrown around is that 98% of people who purchase an information product never put the advice into action. I don't know what the stats are for supplements, but I imagine most people don't take their supplements as regularly as they need to get results.

Nevertheless, if you're product is good and you make enough sales, these victory stories will come in.

The best place to get these stories is from *unsolicited* testimonials. Often times, companies will incentivize their customers to give positive reviews on Amazon or other places by offering a discount or free product or something like that. While that can be a valid strategy for earning higher rankings or bolstering your Amazon listing, it's usually not a good source for stories.

When you *ask* people to leave a testimonial, they think they need to talk about the product so you'll end up with a generic sounding testimonial.

What you really want is people to talk about the *results* that they got, and the *struggle* and *frustrations* that they overcame. Your product is just a missing piece of the puzzle that made it all come together for them.

That's why **unsolicited thank you's are the best source of customer hero stories**. Capture the story at the moment of victory.

Also, when the feedback is unsolicited, it's probably already in sharable form. You just need to get permission to share and maybe trim out some of the extraneous details.

Communicating in stories is our natural way of sharing information. It's only when we get "serious" and try to sit down to write that we lose touch with our natural storyteller.

In most cases, you can just paraphrase or even quote what your customer said to you. But if you need to rearrange it a little bit to make it more compelling story, just remember that formula I showed you earlier:

1. Character
2. Desire
3. Conflict

If you have those three elements, you have a story. But in this case, you're also going to talk about the *victory* as well. This is a success story, not a tragedy. The success at the end is what makes it inspirational.

Using Other People's Success Stories to Sell Your Product

Here's one final trick you can use if you need to "cheat" a bit. Sometimes you don't have enough of these stories from your own customers so you need to borrow from other sources.

Like I showed in earlier chapters, you can borrow stories from Reddit or other forums. People share success stories in there as well as their struggles. So all you have to do is find a success story, paraphrase it, and then explain how their journey would have been easier if they had your solution.

> Subj: Husband has a new girlfriend
>
> I recently read about a woman who found herself in a predicament.
>
> Her husband was a member of a club that meets every month. She normally didn't go because they talk about boring guy stuff (like electronics and sports).
>
> But she's checked out a couple of their events, so his friends knew her at least a little bit.
>
> One day, her husband is cornered by a couple of his friends...
>
> "WTF happened to your marriage?! Is everything okay?"
>
> At first her husband thinks they're teasing so he laughs. Then it hits him:
>
> They're dead serious.
>
> They saw him at the last meeting with a different woman.

Customers on Demand

At least, that's what they thought.

See, they hadn't seen her since the last summer... when she really did look like a different woman.

(She were wondering why all those guys seemed so uncomfortable talking to you at the last meeting...)

Her husband pulls out his phone and shows several of her progress pictures to prove to his friends that, indeed, it still is her!

This is one of the great drawbacks of losing so much weight in a short time span... your husband is going to have to constantly prove to his concerned friends that he really is still with the same woman :-)

You might be thinking this is just fantasy, but you truly can become a new woman by effectively burning off fat.

But why do so many women struggle to lose weight?

It really is heartbreaking that so many women do not know the truth about effective weight loss. They blame themselves, telling themselves things like:

- *"I'm overeating."*
- *"I'm not getting enough exercise."*
- *"I'm just not disciplined enough!"*
- *"I'm just too lazy. I'll never lose this weight!"*

While exercise and proper eating are important, more often than not, it is hormonal barriers that prevent women from losing weight.

These hormonal barriers (such as ghrelin and leptin imbalances) will sabotage your efforts to lose weight no matter how hard you try to stick with your diet and exercise plan.

> The good news is this little-known problem has a simple solution. The video below will show you 3 simple strategies for restoring your hormone balance so you can (1) burn fat easily and (2) have more energy throughout the day.
>
> Check it out **here**:
>
> LINK

This is a sneaky but ethical way you can use other people's success stories to sell your own product. So long as you empathize with the problem you can still present your offer as the best solution even if the character didn't actually use your product.

People have an unlimited appetite for inspirational stories, so the only limit to this strategy is the number of inspirational success stories that you can find. And the more stories you share, the more offers you can make, and the more of your product you will sell.

~9~
The Dopamine Hit

People literally live for dopamine.

Dopamine is the chemical in the brain that makes us happy. Without dopamine, there would be no pleasure or purpose in life and we'd have no reason to live. We all seek out dopamine hits.

If you can tie your product into such an experience, your market will not only want to buy it, they will become addicted after using it. This addiction does not come from a chemical substance in the product, but rather **they become addicted because of the progress and the results that it helps them achieve.**

And, as far as dopamine is concerned, progress equals happiness. Momentum is the chemical high of life.

When you link your product to dopamine, you are repositioning yourself from a company that is just selling a product to a friend that is talking about a shared passion with your readers. If you are giving people dopamine hits in a non-harmful way, you are literally creating happiness in their life.

Dopamine is also what makes your product "stick" after the first purchase. Because, as you probably know, the real money is made not on the first sale; it's made on subscriptions and repeated purchases of people paying month after month after they become "hooked" on the goodness you offer.

Another great thing about this message strategy is you don't have to find a story to use it. Sometimes, you're supply of good stories is running low, but you still want to send out an offer. With this strategy, you can create content on demand and you can do this unlimited times. I'll show you what I mean in a second.

Dopamine: Hit Me Up with the Good Stuff

Dopamine, to put it in simple terms, is the chemical that is triggered in our brains when we make progress towards a visual goal or find something useful.

As far as you're concerned, dopamine is why **people have an instinctive need to collect tips and information that helps them advance towards their goals.**

Dopamine is the entire reason that the information product industry exists. People get a dopamine hit every time they find information that has potential to help them solve a problem. In fact, this chemical is so appealing that it can create an unusual problem where someone will continue to buy information products over and over again and never use the information. They are just living for the "high" they get whenever they discover a new information product.

You can see a similar behavior with people who buy supplements. I know people who have dozens of supplements in their cupboard. They try out everything that's sounds like it might be good. Then they stop using it when the next thing comes along or when the excitement of the imagined results wears off.

I'm not saying this dopamine-driven purchasing is good or bad. I'm just saying you have to realize this is why people make that first purchase of a supplement or a health product. **They get excited by discovering something new and useful.**

So here's an example how you can use a dopamine-inducing tip to sell your product:

> **Subj: How to eat healthy at restaurants**
>
> I get asked variations of this question all the time:
>
> "I'm very busy and don't have time to eat at home all the time. Avoiding eating out is almost impossible. Do you have any tips on staying healthy while eating out?"
>
> While I recommend all my clients eat at home as much as they can, I do understand the difficulties.
>
> In fact, just last week I was attending a 4-day conference in Atlanta. Being away from my kitchen disrupts the routine. I'd be lying if I said I remained perfectly faithful to my diet :-)
>
> Thankfully, I do have a few tricks up my sleeves for dealing with situations like this.
>
> One thing I do a lot is eat at Chipotle's. They have quality ingredients and I never feel bloated or sluggish after eating there.
>
> Healthy eating is catching on, especially among the entrepreneur crowd, so if you're out doing business, it's often an easy sell to choose a healthy (but tasty) option over going out for greasy food.
>
> If Chipotle's is not an option, I use an app called Cheat Day which allows to quickly look up the calories and other information for whatever restaurant the group is attending. The app automatically shows the menu items with the fewest calories first

so it makes decisions a snap. (No one wants to be the one holding up the line 'cause you're trying to make calculations on the spot.)

These are just a couple of techniques I use. In next month's [NEWSLETTER], the entire issue is devoted to readers favorite strategies for staying healthy while on the go. You don't want to miss this one.

Subscribe here:

LINK

Tips for Creating Tips

The simplest way to come up with an exciting tip is to simply to **connect your product to a universal desire**. I'm going to talk about how to do this in more detail in a later chapter. But for now, let's take the universal desire of sex as an example...

People want to be able to express themselves sexually, but if they are not healthy or if they lack energy, they're not going to be able to do that. So even if your product is not about sex directly, you could still give them a hot tip on how to increase their libido or how to have more energy in the bedroom.

After you give the tip, you simply tie it into your product. You could say how your product makes the tip easier to implement. Or if you're selling an information product, you could say this is just one of many tips that you cover in the full product.

However you do it, you want to make the email about the tip, not about your product. Your readers will fill in the blank themselves. All you have to do is drop the hint that your product can help them implement the tip.

If you master the art of creating juicy tips, you will literally have an unlimited number of compelling emails you can send to your list.

You can also use this strategy on other platforms as well such as Facebook or Google. With a little bit of creativity, you can tie your product to almost anything and broadcast those tips on any platform.

And once again, more messages = more offers = more sales.

It's as simple as that.

Part III:

Making the Perfect Pitch

~10~
The Daily "Mini-Sales Letter"

If you're a lazy marketer, you'll *love* email.

Putting together a full-blown promotion is a lot of work. You got to find a killer hook, create a bunch of ads to test, get the tracking right, write a great sales page, etc. If you nail it, you'll hit it big. But until you do, marketing can be a lot of hard and frustrating work.

This is why I find it ironic that companies who spend so much money and effort creating a killer promotion neglect to maximize the value from their customer lists with emails. Emails are so easy compared to other kinds of marketing. Write a story. Drop a link. Make some money.

Yet so few people do that. Or if they do, they don't mail their list nearly enough.

I call these "mini-sales letters" because that's exactly what they are. It's a quick letter to your list that shares something interesting and then invites them to check out your product. A good sales letter is never boring to read. In fact, your readers shouldn't even realize that they're reading a sales letter because it's so fun to read.

These mini-sales letters I'm showing you how to create are going to be on point with your readers' problems, frustrations & desires. If you do it right, they won't even think of it like a sales letter. We just call it a sales letter because it's designed to make you sales. But when your market is reading it, they just think of it as interesting content or a newsletter.

Email allows you to send **unlimited messages at near-zero cost**. Why wouldn't you take advantage of that opportunity?

Yes, I know many marketers have abused this opportunity. When people hear about sending an email every single day, they think it's about spamming people. They get skeptical because they're thinking about those marketers who send out a hard pitch every day. Stuff like that just burns out your list and they'll unsubscribe. But that's not at all what I'm talking about.

What I'm talking about is sending an interesting message that your market is going to love to read. Then you just plug to your product message... *like talk radio.*

You can send as many of these as you want and you're not going to be limited by click costs or have to worry about violating platform policies or things like that.

How to "Get Away" With Selling Every Day

A mini sales letter is, as the name implies, similar to a full length sales letter but much shorter. It's simply a compelling story with a soft sell or a plug to your product page at the end.

Because these mini-sales letters are so short (and fun to read), it allows you to

**Send an offer to your list every single day
or even multiple times a day!**

The more you send out your offer, the more sales you make. It's as simple as that.

People have a limited tolerance for sales pitches, but they have an *unlimited* appetite for stories and entertainment. After people come home from a tiring day of work, what do they do? They sit down and binge watch Netflix. People can consume entertainment for hours. If anything, we have to work at disciplining ourselves to *limit* the amount of entertainment we consume.

If your marketing messages are entertaining, they can be a pleasant distraction from their boring work.

Another thing to keep in mind:

Timing is everything when it comes to sales. Someone might be fully persuaded that your product is good. They may believe it will help them solve their problem. But they may just not be ready to pull the trigger. Maybe they have another priority. Maybe they're waiting for their last paycheck to clear. Whatever the case, there's a lot of reasons why people will feel that it's not the right time to act. But later on they'll be ready to take action (if they remember you).

If you're showing up every day in their inbox with a fun and compelling message, you're going to stay at the top of their mind and so when they're ready to buy. They'll see your latest email and think *"Oh yeah. I wanted to get this."*

Honestly, they may not even read your email if they're ready to buy. They'll just scroll down to the bottom, click the link, and buy your product. They're already pre-sold. And your last offer happened to show up at the right time.

Anatomy of an Invisible Sales Letter

Let's take a look at how to structure these mini-sales letters.

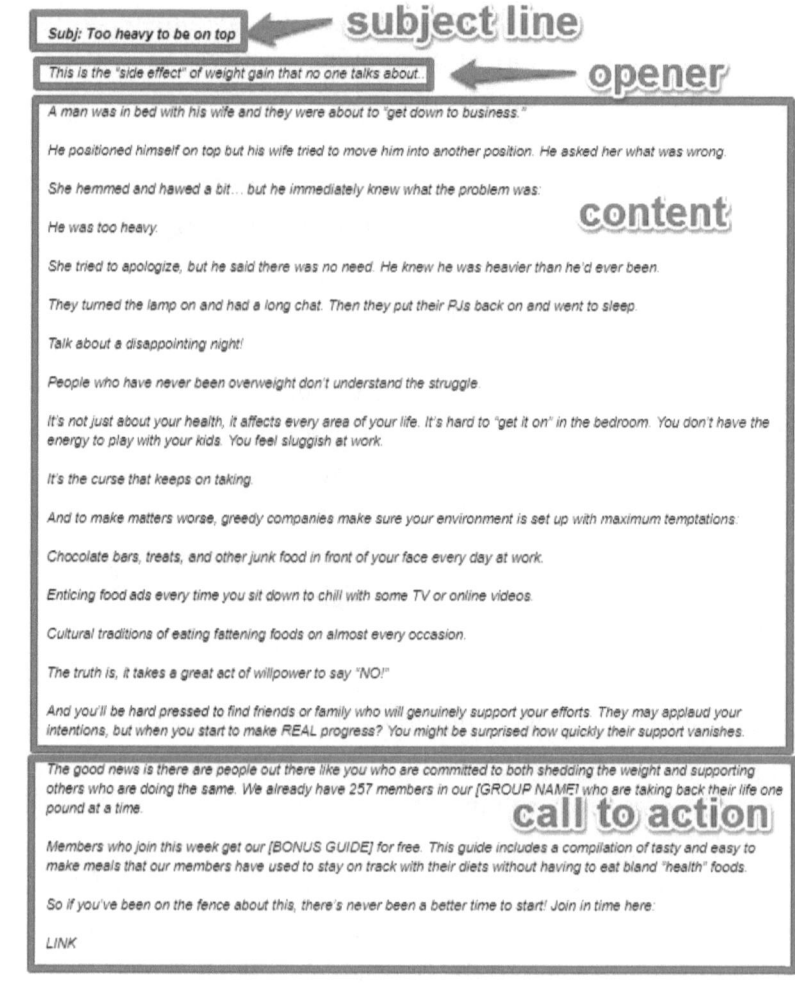

One important thing you should be aware of:

When you email your list every day, you are going to get some people that unsubscribe. You may even get a few complaints. And that's okay. As the great email marketer Ben Settle says, daily emails are about

**Playing to win
rather than playing to not lose**.

If someone is going to get offended that you appended a call to action and a link at the bottom of your free tip, that's not the type of person you want on your list anyway. They're never going to buy your product anyway so it's best for everyone that they get off your list.

You can only deposit money. Your bank doesn't care about the size of your email list.

Also, if someone doesn't want to be informed every day about a solution to their problem, then that's a sign that they're not really serious about solving it. If someone was serious about solving their problem, they would have either bought your product by now (in which case you would segment them onto a new list and offer them something else) or they're still "on the fence" and they're reading your emails to judge whether your solution is right for them.

But if someone is just going to sign up for a freebie and then not want to read your emails, they're not going to be a buyer so it's perfectly fine that these people leave your list.

In fact, getting people *off* your list is one reason this system works so well. When you purge people from your list that aren't serious about buying, you end up with a hot list of people who are passionate about solving their problem. These are the people who very likely convert to a customer for you at some point.

Become an "Idea Machine"

Another challenge people run into with this system is **how do you come up with fresh ideas every day?**

Fear not; there are ways to do this.

I gave you some examples in the previous section with the five basic messaging strategies. If you want more ideas, check out Ben Settle (BenSettle.com). Ben's the guy who originally taught me the daily infotainment strategy. He has a great newsletter called *Email Players* that is filled with ideas on how to spin your knowledge of your market into unlimited emails.

The bottom line is if you have a good offer and you understand your market, doubling or tripling your sales is a simple matter of sending more offers. In these next few chapters, I'll show you specific ways to attach your offers to your infotaining email content.

Let's dive in...

~11~
Sex Up the Offer

People do not care how good your product is until they see it as a means to get something they strongly desire. Every purchase anyone ever makes is because they had the *desire* to achieve something.

In many cases, this desire is unspoken by both the customer and the marketer. The customer fills in the desire in his own head and then buys the product. But imagine how powerful it could be if you could trigger these powerful desires in your prospect's minds before they buy?

It's a frustrating experience to have a perfect product and yet no one buys it. They don't buy because they do not see the benefit to themselves.

If you can tie your product to your prospect's strongest desires, your product becomes irresistible.

The truth is, most people do not believe that they can get what they truly desire in life. Their friends and family doubt them, they put them down for being "unrealistic", and they often struggle with self-doubt themselves.

Marketing is about giving people hope. It's about being the one person that believes in them and says, "You can achieve your goal. You can achieve your desire." It's not about manipulating people, it's about positioning your product in a way where people see it as just one tool on their way to achieving their dreams.

I'm going to assume for the sake of this book that you are selling a high quality product. There are charlatans out there that use people's desires to manipulate them and sell crappy products. This doesn't help anyone because it's just making people more skeptical and distrustful of marketers. But when you do this ethically (i.e. don't lie or over-hype your product), you really are helping people change their lives and move one step closer to fulfilling their dreams.

10 Ways to Make Your Offer Sexy

When I talk about "sexing up the offer", I mean that you don't start with your product like most marketers do. Instead, you start with something that people strongly (and often secretly) desire. The desire is so integrated into the core of their being that when you talk about it, they immediately perk up and pay attention.

Again, remember that

> **People aren't looking for products to buy,
> they want to fulfill their secret dreams and aspirations.**

If a they believe a product will help them to achieve that, they are very likely to buy it.

So what are these desires you can tie your product to? I find Napoleon Hill's 10 Basic Human Desires to be a good list to start with:

- The desire for sex expression and love
- The desire for physical food
- The desire for spiritual, mental, and physical self-expression
- The desire for perpetuation of life after death
- The desire for power over others
- The desire for material wealth
- The desire for knowledge
- The desire to imitate others
- The desire to excel others
- The seven basic fears
  - Fear of poverty
  - Fear of criticism
  - Fear of ill health
  - Fear of the loss of love
  - Fear of the loss of liberty
  - Fear of old age
  - Fear of death

Any Product Can Get a Makeover

You might read that list above and think, *"My product doesn't relate to all of those."*

Well, here's a little secret:

Health is related to *everything*.

If you don't have energy, you can't sexually express yourself like you want. If you're overweight, it'll be difficult to get respect.

Whatever you're trying to do, it's all tied to health. If you have a health problem, that's going to affect everything. Selling in the health niche gives you a wide range of private desires you can utilize in your marketing.

Another challenge you might run into is *"which desire do I choose?"*

The great thing about doing a daily email is you don't even have to choose one desire. Just pick any of them, write an email about it, send it out, and see what happens.

Email is not like doing a big promotion like a direct mail or even a Facebook or Google ad campaign where you have to pick one hook and drive everyone through that same message.

Email allows you test an unlimited number of hooks and messages without any loss if it doesn't work. I remember the great humorist Scott Adams (of Dilbert fame) once saying that people only have to find you funny 20% of the time for them to them to consider you an entertaining person. I think a similar rule of thumb applies to email:

> **If you're interesting at least 20% of the time,
> your readers will be hooked.**

And if you talk about the universal desires listed in this chapter, you're practically guaranteed to be interesting. These desires are universal. You can't go wrong with talking about sex, money, self-expression, etc. All these things are going to be immediately relevant to people because everybody wants them.

Write for the Market, Not the Censors

Email is a medium that allows you to talk about almost whatever you want without fear of being censored. Email is a private and, for the most part, uncensored medium. Obviously, you don't want to be offensive to your market. You need to know what's appropriate. For instance, if you're writing to young men trying to increase their testosterone, you'll want to write with hard-hitting energy and even use explicit language. But if you're writing for conservative boomer women, you'll need to be more modest and indirect when talking about the universal desires.

But whatever the case, email allows your *market* to determine what's appropriate to write rather than the policies of Google, Facebook, or whatever platform you're advertising on. Because at the end of the day, it's about your market, not the platform.

What if your readers viewed your product not merely as a way to get healthy but as a way to fulfill their dreams? Do you think some more money might start flowing your way? I think so.

~12~
"Vision Drives Decision"

"Vision drives decision" is the most important sales lesson I learned from the great negotiator Jim Camp. Ambiguity and abstractions do not sell.

If your prospect cannot *picture* the problem that your product solves, they won't understand it. If they don't understand it, they won't buy it, because people don't buy solutions for products that they don't know they have.

The reality is many people have problems that they aren't even fully aware of. **They know they have *frustrations*, but they don't know what the *problem* is.** They drift through life not having any clear direction, struggling to make decisions, simply because they don't have a clear picture of what's at the root of their frustrations.

You do not want your market to be in a state of indecision. Indecisive people do *decide* to use your product. At best, they might *try* it then give up, cancel the subscription, not order the second bottle, whatever the case may be.

As a marketer, you can help your market to get clarity and direction in their life, particularly with their health. You might think you're only selling a product, but really you are helping them to solve a more fundamental problem that perhaps they are not even fully aware of. Creating vision is what allows you to take control of that narrative.

A lot of marketers take a defensive strategy, as if it's a trial at a court of law and they're trying to prove that their product does everything they claim it does. They're dealing with objections. And the people who are watching are simply coming up with more and more doubts and questions and reasons not to buy.

But when you lead with a vision and give them a clear picture of the problem, you're in control of the frame. You're not trying to prove anything about your products. There's no objections because you never even made a claim. **You're simply pointing out the problem, and then your prospect infers that your product can help them solve their problem.**

"More Gore"

Ben Settle, one of my copywriting mentors, would always advise his clients to add "more gore" to their emails. What he meant by that is don't just talk about the problems in an abstract way. *Show them* a frightening picture of what will happen if they don't solve the problem.

People don't react to dangers they can't see. One you've identified the root of the problem, you need to dramatize it. Make it tangible.

Here's one of my favorite examples from Jim Camp:

Say you're trying to convince a friend to wear a seatbelt. You can cite statistics that prove the risk factor, you can argue how easy it is to use seatbelts, you can cite the penalties for not wearing one, etc. etc.

But what Jim Camp would say is

> **"Where do you think your body will end up when your car collides with another at 50 miles per hour?"**

End of discussion. No need to argue.

Data Doesn't Change the Heart

One temptation a lot of people have, especially in the health market, is to lead with the scientific facts and the studies to prove the effectiveness of your product.

There is a place for using these studies, and I'll talk about this later. You want to have proof. You want to have the science give you credibility, but **the science is not what sells your product**. It's the desire and it's the vision of the problem that sells the product.

You want to tie your product to a strong desire, like we talked about in the last chapter. Then you want to give a vision of how a particular problem is threatening to take away something they desire.

As you're learning more about your market, always be mindful of problems. When you're reading studies, pay attention to what is the root problem, and then think how can you turn that into a vision.

Every problem is an opportunity to create a vision that your product can solve. If your prospect can see that vision, they will sell themselves. You won't have to do the selling.

Imagine how great it'd be if you didn't even have to make claims to sell your product. No more worrying about the FTC cracking down on you. **The more you talk about problems instead of solutions, the more your readers will sell themselves, and the less you have to claim**. That, in my opinion, is a superior way of selling.

~13~
No B.S.

It's very popular in the health market to seek out doctors' endorsements for your products. This is for obvious reasons. If you get a doctor's endorsement, it adds credibility to your product. You're not just some random company trying to sell a magic pill for a profit. It actually comes across as a legitimate product.

But what do you do if you don't have a doctor's endorsement?

In many cases, what I'm going to show you is actually *more effective* than a doctor's endorsement because you're helping the reader understand *why* it works instead of asking them to blindly trust a doctor's endorsement. Because, let's face it: people can be skeptical of even doctor's claims. Anyone can claim to be a doctor or maybe the doctor "sold out" or something. There's always reasons to be skeptical of this kind of marketing.

But I'm going to show you how to give proof in a way that your readers both enjoy and creates genuine belief.

When you give proof and explain the mechanism of how your product works, you're showing your readers that you don't think they're stupid. You're not just telling them to blindly put their trust in you or a doctor. You're telling them, *"I know you're a smart and educated consumer. You don't want to buy anything just because it sounds exciting. You want to know if and how it works."*

This is why you explain the science behind your product. They want the proof. They want to *believe* your product will get them the results they want.

When you sell in this way, you're doing it in a way that feels like education to them. But not the boring kind of education associated with school. This kind of education is interesting to them because it's about solving their problems. You're giving them a mini-science lesson to help them understand their bodies and how to make it function like they want.

People like to learn about science, especially when it's relevant to a problem that they're solving. It can be difficult to incorporate scientific concepts into your sales copy, but I'm going to show you how to do it in a way that is fun and easy to read without losing the authority of the "hard science."

How to Create Belief

The key to creating belief is to explain the *mechanism* of how your product works. A mechanism, in the health market, is the scientific explanation for why your supplement, diet, or whatever you're promoting works.

Since we're talking about *physical* results, we usually want to explain the mechanism with scientific terminology. While it is not necessary to have a scientific explanation to know or prove something works, the scientific language helps us feel comfortable that it's the real deal rather than some kind of quack remedy.

Neither does the science make your readers want your product. You first need the desire and the vision like we talked about previously.

But once they get to that point where they want to believe, they're going to be skeptical. They don't want to be a sucker and get ripped off by some online scam. So they ask questions like, *"Is this legit? It seems too good to be true…"*

Science is what alleviates those doubts. If something is scientific, we feel confident that it conforms with what we know about reality. This is what separates your products in their minds as a real viable solution rather than some crazy "alternative" gamble.

As an example of this, let's say you wanted to persuade someone about the power of "positive thinking." You could show examples successful people who believe in positive thinking. You could quote mantras like "more smiling, less worrying" or "Be grateful. Be positive. Be true. Be kind."

But none of that will be as effective as something like this:

> *The human brain runs on electrical pulses. Brain waves are measured in electron volts. Electrons are a form of energy.*
>
> *This is another way of saying "thoughts are things." Thoughts have a real physical existence. And thanks to modern technology we can observe and measure them (to a certain extent.)*
>
> *Physicists tell us when two electric waves strike each other, they will combine. If both waves have the same charge (either positive or negative) they will merge together to form a stronger, more energetic wave. This is known as* **constructive interference**.

*Likewise, if two electric waves with opposite charges strike each other, they will cancel each other out. This is known as **destructive interference**.*

Since our thoughts are (physically speaking) waves of electric energy, they follow the same laws of physics.

These laws are easy to observe for ourselves. When we are interacting with someone with a positive outlook on a topic, whatever positive thoughts we have about the topic are amplified. Likewise, when we interact with someone who is expressing pessimism, bitterness, envy, or other such things, our own negative thoughts will be amplified.

Like joins with like and amplifies itself.

*In short, this is known as the **law of attraction**.*

Notice how much more believable something is when it's explained in terms of science? In many cases, seeing evidence is not enough. We want to understand *why* and *how* it works before we're ready to believe it.

Or even if we already believed something, hearing a scientific explanation will strengthen our belief in the mechanism.

Ditch the Techno-babble

An important caveat to giving proof is that you have to make it understandable to reader. If you just throw out a bunch of scientific jargon, it's going to confuse them. If they're confused, they're not going to buy.

You want to understand the science behind it, but you also want to use metaphors or examples that make it easy for ordinary people to understand. Most people are not versed in scientific literature. They don't study science beyond high school in most cases. Even what they did learn in school, they probably forgot all that.

You still want to use the key terms because that's what gives a sense of authority to the mechanism. But you need to wrap those terms in a metaphor so your readers can visualize and understand it.

The best example I've ever seen of this is an explainer video created by Russell Brunson for the company Pruvit. The video is about ketosis, a topic that can be difficult to understand for ordinary people who don't understand how it works.

At the time of this writing, you can watch the video for yourself on Pruvit's YouTube channel. Look for a video titled, "KETO//OS Explained."

In case the video is taken down by time you read this, here's an excerpt:

> *Have you ever built a campfire before?*
>
> *If so, did you know that by building that fire, you actually unlocked the power for unlimited energy, fat loss, and focus?*
>
> *Let me explain...*
>
> *When you build a campfire, there are three types of fuel that you can use:*
>
> *1. Kindling*

2. *Logs*
3. *Coal*

The kindling is the easiest to catch on fire. It burns fast and, if you're not careful, it will be gone before the larger logs even catch on fire.

The logs take a little longer to catch on fire, but if you're able to burn them correctly, eventually they'll be able to catch the coals on fire that will give you a nice long heat that will keep you warm throughout the night.

So how does knowing that give you unlimited energy, fat loss, and focus?

Well, did you know there are also three types of fuel that run in your body?

1. *Carbs*
2. *Proteins*
3. *Fats*

And each one works differently inside of you…

He then goes on to explain how ketosis works by comparing each energy source to the campfire analogy. Being in ketosis is burning fats, which is like the long-burning coal in the campfire.

Don't Bury Your Readers with Proof

Another thing to be careful of is you don't want to pile on the proof in an email. A great tip I picked up from Oren Klaff, author of *Pitch Anything*, is that the last item on a list is what sticks in people's minds. So if you give people a big list of proof, the last thing you say is what they're going to remember. And, in many cases, the last item of proof we give is not the strongest point. So it's best to just pick your *strongest* point of proof and *only* present that.

The email should be a quick and easy read. It's not about dumping a lot of scientific information. You're just picking one simple mechanism to highlight. In many cases, all you need is a sentence or two to add some believability.

When you're selling a product, you're not trying to make a scientific case. Your readers already want to believe. They just need that little bit of proof thrown in the mix to reassure them that they are making a smart and informed decision.

When you can explain the science in a way that people understand, you're going to feel good about selling your product. There's just something about having science back your products. Even if you know from experience that it works, if you have a solid scientific backing and you can show that to people, that gives you a lot of confidence to promote your product without fear of looking like a quack or someone peddling magic pills or anything like that.

~14~
Don't Kill the Sale

Making an offer is a delicate art. The sale can be killed by either making the offer too soon or by not making it soon enough. But if you know your buyer's level of awareness, you can sell to them in a way that feels natural and won't irritate them.

In many cases, you can increase your sales simply by changing *when* you reveal the offer.

If your product is...

- Expensive
- Hard to understand
- High commitment

… then it will make more sense to send people to long-form content like a pre-sell page, article, video, webinar registration, booking a consultation, etc.

On the other hand, if your product is…

- Inexpensive (less than $100)
- Easy to understand
- Low commitment

… then you will probably get better results by sending people straight to the product or sales page.

People hate to be educated when they're ready to buy. They also hate to be shown an offer when they're skeptical. You've got to find the right balance between the two and give them just enough information; not too much, not too little.

When you're selling supplements, people already understand what they are. They've been doing it for years. They probably have dozens of other supplements they've bought before. So you don't really need to explain the product per se. You just need to build trust that your product works. The emails that you've been sending them build the trust. So in most cases, you can send them straight to the product page to order without needing to provide much additional information.

(Side note: If you're selling a supplement on Amazon, daily emails linked to your Amazon page can be a great way to increase your sales velocity and move up to Page 1 quickly.)

If you're selling a newsletter or other information product, your readers may need a bit more information before they're ready to buy. Although they understand what a newsletter is in a physical sense, they may not understand what it will help them accomplish or why they need it on a monthly basis. So there's a lot more nuances that need to be understood before they're ready to commit to a newsletter. So in that case linking your emails out to a long form sales letter or even a video sales letter might make more sense.

When in Doubt, Do Less

If your sales page is getting a lot of visitors from your emails, but not many sales, you may want to switch up how you present the offer. If you've been going straight to the offer and people aren't buying, try adding a little bit of presale information. Maybe share a story or add some bullet points to your sales page.

But if in doubt, try going straight for the sale. Honestly, the emails are going to do the heavy lifting for you. The emails are the pre-sale. So by the time they land on your sales page, they're 90% sold. You're more likely to lose sales by not getting to the point about the offer than you are by showing the offer too soon. Your readers already know you have something for sale because you've been plugging the product in every email so they're not going to be turned off by seeing a price and a "buy" button.

Don't make things harder for yourself than you need to. Emails can do the heavy lifting of the preselling. And in most cases, a simple sales page or even an order page is all you need to get the job done effectively.

Part IV:

Resources

~15~
How to Get Started

At this stage, you should have a solid understanding of the fundamentals of email marketing. You should have a clear sense of the power of infotainment and how it can be used to multiply your sales.

A competent email marketer will be able to:

- Find insights about your perfect market and spin those insights into infotaining emails
- Come up with an unlimited number of compelling themes for your emails
- Send emails *every day* without boring the readers
- Pre-sell the offer by blending compelling content with an intriguing call-to-action
- Multiply sales without requiring additional advertising (the ultimate goal)

You have two options for executing this system:

1. Do it yourself
2. Hire a copywriter

If you do it yourself, all you have to pay for is an email broadcasting service. The price of these services depends on the size of your list, but you shouldn't need to pay more than $100/m in most cases.

If you hire a good copywriter to do this for you, you'll need to pay anywhere from $5K-$15K or so per month in most cases. But the advantage is you don't have to do a thing other than write the checks. Instead of paying that money to Google or Facebook to promote an idea that may or may not be profitable, **a good email copywriter will start multiplying your sales immediately**.

As an email copywriter myself, my mission is to multiply sales by sending a daily compelling email that addresses your perfect market's pain points and interests. I do everything on your behalf, including the market research and idea generation. I can write in someone else's voice and turn other media (such as podcasts or videos) into compelling emails that make you more sales. Your time commitment is minimal. All you have to do is send me links to existing resources and tell me who to send the copy to so he can load it into your email system.

If you're interested in learning more about my service, simply look in the next chapter for my contact information.

The next step in the process is to schedule a brief phone consultation with me where you'll tell me more about your situation and I'll be able to determine if/how I can help you.

I only take on clients who are in a situation who can afford a good copywriter. If your revenue is under 6-figures, my service is not for you. If you're already bringing in at least $500K in annual revenue, a service like this might be a perfect fit for you.

To contact me, simply refer to the next chapter for my contact information.

~16~
Author Contact Information

If you'd like to take the next step to see if I can help multiply your sales through email marketing, simply contact me for a free initial consultation.

I'll evaluate your current situation and challenges you'd like to address to see if I'm able to meet your objectives.

To request a free consultation, simply email me at Levi@LeviTheEmailGuy.com or leave a voicemail at **208-495-6119**.

www.ingramcontent.com/pod-product-compliance
Lightning Source LLC
Chambersburg PA
CBHW030903180526
45163CB00004B/1679